Maggie —
This just had your name on it when I found it? Enjoy!

Love,
Vicky

I *Purr,*

Never Before

Therefore

Collected Observations

I Am

On All Things Cat

MERRIT MALLOY

Price Stern Sloan, Inc.
a member of
The Putnam Berkley Group, Inc.
New York

Jacket Photo: Animals Animals
Copyright © 1994 Terence Gili
Interior Illustrations by Ellen Laning

Copyright © 1994 by Merrit Malloy
Illustrations Copyright © 1994 by Price Stern Sloan, Inc.
Published by Price Stern Sloan, Inc.
a member of
The Putnam Berkley Group, Inc.
200 Madison Avenue, New York, NY 10016

Library of Congress Card Catalog Number 94-7563

Library of Congress Cataloging-in-Publication Data

I purr, therefore I am: never before collected observations on all
things cat / (compiled by) Merrit Malloy
p.   cm.
ISBN 0-8431-3782-7
1.   Cats— Quotations, maxims, etc.   I. Malloy, Merrit.
PN6084.C23I2   1994
636.8—dc20   94-7563   CIP

Printed in the United States of America

1 2 3 4 5 6 7 8 9 10

This book is printed on acid-free paper.
∞

Dedication

I was never owned by a cat until I met James. He became my partner on these pages. He was loyal, in spite of his inability to be at all reliable.

James didn't play up to me, but he did often surprise me with his unexpected visits to my writing desk where he rubbed up against me and climbed under my working hand and folded into my body for his afternoon nap.

Mankind, being the species that writes, is far more quotable than the cat, but I suspect not nearly as eloquent. This book is for you, my eloquent, unrepeatable James.

Acknowledgement

This book is the result of my tenacious and spirited partners at Price Stern Sloan, Leonard Stern, Bob Lovka, and Tiffany Young, who kept this book on track even when there was no road.

Preface

Being owned by a cat is a humbling experience.
It forces you to notice at least once a day that,
in the actual scheme of things, we humans are
not the only creatures of distinctive value on
the planet.

Being owned by a cat is a serious nuisance.
It demands a certain order to life that is often
most unsettling. It forces us, much too often, to
simply STOP and BE there. These little creatures
have a genius for creating small landscapes of
peace and solitude. This truly can interfere with
"real life" and mess up our oh-so important
agendas. We make plans, we write lists, we set
goals, we go to seminars...and cats laugh. Out of
nowhere they jump into you, not just onto your
lap, but into YOU. They stop your busy work
with an invitation to join, to be, to listen.

The thoughts, quips and quotes of this little
book attempt to bring that elusive being known
as CAT into focus and to delight and chuckle
over all those things uniquely cat. Here, in this
collection of new, rare and previously unanth-
ologized thoughts and quotes, you will find your
cat and a number of cats you know. From the
stalking to the stretching to the purring to the
flopping onto the middle of the papers you
spread before you, this whimsical collection
comes alive as 'cat' and celebrates a unique
spirit, one that proudly proclaims, "I Purr,
Therefore I Am!"

—MERRIT MALLOY

A cat stretches from one end of my childhood to the other.

—BLAGA DIMITROVA

Cats are dogs with a college education.

—GRACE HODGSON

I gave my cat a bath the other day...he loves it. He sat there, he enjoyed it, it was fun for me. The fur would stick to my tongue, but other than that...

—STEVE MARTIN

Friends may come and go, but cats accumulate.

—BOB MCMAHON

*A cat gets into everything...
including your conscience.*

—LAURA INGINERI

*I can't decide if I have a cat
or a cat has me.*

—ESTHER MARTON

*You can't own a cat. The best
you can do is be partners.*

—SIR HARRY SWANSON

*C*ats are God's way of saying,
"Gotcha!"

—O'BRIAN "MAC" WIEST

All loyalty has a little fur in it.

—M. MALLOY

*Don't mess with your cat
when you're stoned.
He'll give you a look like,
"Give it your best shot, man,
I've been doing catnip since
the day I was born!"*

—ROBIN WILLIAMS

*Cats are smarter than dogs.
You can't get eight cats to
pull a sled through snow.*

—WILL CUPPY

*In nine lifetimes, you'll
never know as much about
your cat as your cat knows
about you.*

—MICHAEL ZULLO

A cat can be trusted to purr when she is pleased, which is more than can be said for human beings.

—WILLIAM RALPH INGE

In my house lives a cat who is a curmudgeon and cantankerous, a cat who is charming and convivial, and a cat who is combative and commendable. And yet I have but one cat.

—DAVE EDWARDS

You can lead a cat to water but you still can't get the horse to drink it.

—CHARLES FITZSIMONS

Cats put me on the purrs of a dilemma. My heart has room for 10, but my allergy won't tolerate one.

—SHERRY LANSING

I have an entrepreneurial cat. He employs kittens to catch his tail.

—E. WEINSTEIN

A cat is a puzzle for which there is no solution.

—HAZEL NICHOLSON

A meow massages the heart.

—STUART MCMILLAN

14

Cats wo...
that isn't us...
—HA...

Cats are endless
opportunities for revelation.
—LESLIE KAPP

My cat constantly rubs against
my leg, making each of us
feel infinitely better.

—ANN PORTER

Cats come and go without
ever leaving.

—MARTHA CURTIS

*Cats know...even before
you do.*

—PAULA JENKS

*The mathematical probability
of a common cat doing
exactly as it pleases is the
one scientific absolute in
the world.*

—LYNN M. OSBAND

Everything comes to those who wait...except a cat.

—MARILYN PETERSON

When you consider that the snow leopard has come to the brink of extinction while the Pekingese has doubled its population this decade, it's obvious that somebody hasn't thought this thing through.

—A. WHITNEY BROWN

The problem with cats is that they get the exact same look on their face whether they see a moth or an ax-murderer.

—PAULA POUNDSTONE

If you call a cat and it comes running, what you have is a dog.

—MAX ADAMS

Cats do care. For example, they know instinctively what time we have to be at work in the morning and they wake us up twenty minutes before the alarm goes off.

—MICHAEL NELSON

Never wear anything that panics the cat.

—P.J. O'ROURKE

A cat can purr its way out of anything.

—DONNA MCCROHAN

Cats are our last best chance to have a dysfunctional relationship.

—JOHN BUSH

*What is unique about cats
is their ability to actually
be themselves.*

—ALISHA EVERETT

*If you don't want a cat to
walk all over you, sleep
standing up!*

—G.W. ESKOW

Cats won't lie on a book that isn't well-written.

—HAROLD WEISS

Ballanchine has taught his cat to perform brilliant jetes and tours en l'air; he says at last he has a body worth choreographing for.

—BERNARD TAPER

If actions speak louder than words, cats are always at the top of their voice.

—FAYE CASTELL

*A cat doesn't take
up much space...and
even less if it has to.*

—JEAN JANSEN

*A walking, prancing,
pouncing, sun-soaking,
sleeping machine.*

—THOMAS GATO

*If dogs could dance, they
would be cats.*

—R.A. LOVKA

25

If a tree falls in the forest and nobody hears it, cats laugh.

—BENNY THALBERG

In life there are two compensations — Prozac and cats.

—BRIAN WALSH

Some cats is blind, and stone-deaf some. But ain't no cat wuz ever dumb.

—A. HENDERSON EUWER

*Cats are femme; dogs
are butch.*

—LAURA BELLOTTI

*All cats are possessed of a
proud spirit, and the surest
way to forfeit the esteem of
a cat is to treat him as an
inferior being.*

—MICHAEL JOSEPH

An ordinary
kitten will
ask more
questions
than
any five
year-old.
—CARL VAN
VECHTEN

*Cats lie, but they don't
give details.*

—SAM GEHRING

*Cats are gymnasts in
fur coats.*

—JOHN FALSEY

*The worst cat I ever had
was wonderful.*

—MARILYN PETERSON

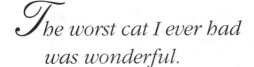

It is useless to punish a cat. They have no conception of human discipline; if they do, the idea is unattractive to them.

—LLOYD ALEXANDER

Dogs teach you how to love. Cats teach you how to live.

—M. MALLOY

A catless writer is almost inconceivable. It's a perverse taste, really, since it would be easier to write with a herd of buffalo in the room than even one cat; they make nests in the notes and bite the end of the pen and walk on the typewriter keys.

—BARBARA HOLLAND

Beware. A gift of milk turns the vagabond cat into a permanent guest.

—BEA POST

Although of alley origin, my cat friend is of careful manner and noble spirit. I believe I have a "Thomas" cat.

—ALVIN OLSON

My cat says nothing.
Maybe a person
got his
tongue.
—DON ADAMS

Cats are
self-employed.
—SY FISCHER

𝒯or the artist, a cat is a still life in motion.

—GLORIA STROOCK

𝒯hree words, feasibility, flexibility, fluidity, have the same definition — cat.

—J. CORWIN

*The way in which she
walks, the way in which
she stalks, the way in which
she "talks," makes even
the most ordinary cat
extraordinary.*

—PETER COLLIER

*This mysterious, mystical
bundle of fur that won't
come when you call it.*

—JOHN REYNOLDS

I'm used to dogs. When you leave them in the morning they stick their nose in the door crack and stand there like a portrait until you turn the key eight hours later. A cat would never put up with that kind of rejection. When you returned, she'd stalk you until you dozed off and then suck the air out of your body.

—ERMA BOMBECK

You can talk a cat into anything he or she already wants to do.

—GEORGE OTTO

The ball, a captured prey. The leaf, a bird in flight. The string, a wiggly adversary. Such is the fantasy life of cats.

—R.A. LOVKA

It is of course, totally pointless to call a cat when it is intent on the chase. They are deaf to the interruptive nonsense of humans. They are on cat business, totally serious and involved.

—JOHN D. MACDONALD

My cat speaks sign language with her tail.

—ROBERT A. STERN

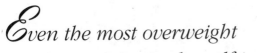

Even the most overweight cat can arrange herself in thin poses.

—MR. BLACKWELL

Cats don't rent. They own.

—TOM POSTON

Dogs come when you call them. Cats screen their calls.

—MELISSA ZIMBALIST

Somehow, cats just happen to you.

—MELODY RHEEMS

Being around cats as a boy taught me to respect women as a man.

—ERIK GREEN

Cats know they're special. That is part of their irresistible fascination.

—DAVID D. DAVIS

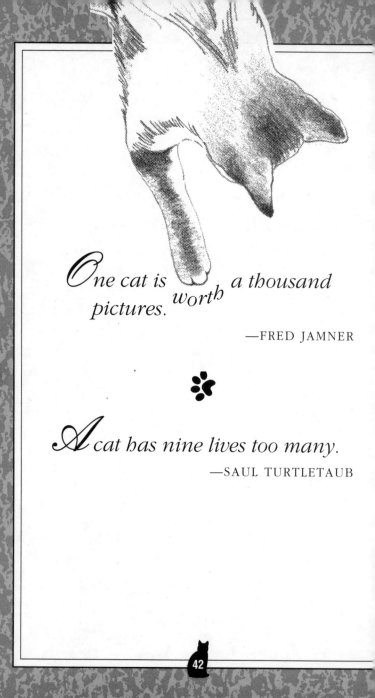

*O*ne cat is *worth* a thousand
pictures.

—FRED JAMNER

A cat has nine lives too many.

—SAUL TURTLETAUB

I had been told that the training procedure with cats was difficult. It's not. Mine had me trained in two days.

—BILL DANA

Cats are discretion. Dogs are tenderness.

—GIORGIO ARMANI

Men are essentially dogs.
Women are essentially cats.

—GEORGE CARLIN

Cats understand every word
we don't say.

—M. MALLOY

Cats live life on the edge —
the edge of the sofa.

—HOLDEN JACOBY

To Willie...
  Who lives in a world I
    cannot enter
  And knows many things
    beyond my perception,
  Whose demands are
    paramount
  And who alone interrupts
    my work as pleases him,
  For he speaks always
    with love
  In pianissimo purrs and
    muted meows.
                —RAYMOND BUSHNELL

45

If only cats grew
into
kittens.
—R.D.
STERN

Cats are okay.
It's the people
they own that
annoy me.
—AUSTIN HUNTER

A man who was loved by 300 women singled me out to live with him. Why? I was the only one without a cat.

—ELAYNE BOOSLER

*T*he best advice I ever got was, "If a cat answers, hang up."

—BENNY THALBERG

I thought cats were shy. No way. They're just ignoring us. We bore cats. And purring is just their way of humming to themselves "Oh boy, LitterMan is going to feed me now."

—NEIL "LITTERMAN" FRANKS

My cat, Stains, has a split personality. Not only does he hear his own music, he can ignore it at the same time.

—MELISSA ZIMBALIST

If a cat spoke, it would say things like, "Hey, I don't see the problem here."

—ROY BLOUNT, JR.

Cats are the Dick Cavett of the animal world.

—MORGAN JEFFRIES

We have a cat that is so insecure it has only four lives.

—MITZI McCALL AND
CHARLIE BRILL

I purr, therefore I am.

—ANONYMOUS

*The difference between a cat
and a dog is a cat can bark
and doesn't.*

—D.J. DODD

Dogs sniff. Cats wink.

—LEONARD STERN

If cats won't talk to you, don't blame them. Find something interesting to say.

—TIFFANY ALETHEA YOUNG

A cat has nine lives and an equal number of personalities.

—ALICE MEADOWS

Cats have instincts; we have advertising.

—JON GOODMAN
Dean, University of Southern California,
MBA Program

All my patients are under the bed.

—DR. LOUIS CAMUTI
Veterinarian

You can't train cats. Even though they are often quite talented, they're much too smart to do tricks.

—SASHA SULLIVAN

Cats are infinitely friendlier than dogs. Have you ever seen a "Beware of the cat" sign?

—LEONARD GRAINGER

Cats are designated friends.

—NORMAN CORWIN

Kittens are constantly forgiven.

—DOUGLAS WILK

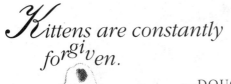

*When a cat chooses you,
you've arrived.*

—JOSH KAPP

*Cats can see your darkest
thoughts.*

—AMY DIAMOND

*A cat had to be involved
in the Declaration of
Independence.*

—GENE LEVITT

If you want to write about mystical reveries and the power of the unknown, have a cat as your collaborator.

—HOWARD BERK

You hush a bark.
You encourage a meow.

—JAY MICHTOM

It is impossible to find a place in which a cat can't hide.

—BILL CARRARO

When dogs leap onto your bed,
it's because they adore being
close to you. When cats leap
onto your bed, it's because
they adore your bed.

—ALISHA EVERETT

You want steady work? Try
getting a cat to roll over.

—MAX ADAMS

Cats are very sincere — even when they don't mean it.

—D.J. DODD

Cats are sculpture set to music.

—M. MALLOY

A new kitten is a bundle of unexpected, unimaginable, friendly trouble.

—MURPHY KALL

Cats have their own agenda. Much of their allure is their mystifying otherness. They're perverse, unpredictable, inscrutable. They're also soft and cuddly.

—LILIAN JACKSON BRAUN

If a cat does something, we call it instinct. If we do the same thing, for the same reason, we call it intelligence.

—WILL CUPPY

❖

Don't worry that your cat doesn't understand what you say; he doesn't care what you're thinking anyway.

—DR. JERI SCHWALB

There's nothing in the world like the affection of an animal. Unfortunately, that's something no cat lover knows about.

—PATRICIA RUSS

Cats think we're just big dogs with can openers.

—MORTON HAY

Having a penis is like owning a cat. What a comedy and what a gift.

—RICHARD RHODES

If you want to know which room in the house is getting sunlight, follow your cat.

—FRED JAMNER

Under the guise of washing each other's ears, cats exchange gossip.

—JANA SUE GILLETTE

Free to good home: female cat or husband. Husband says either he goes or cat goes. Cat fixed, husband isn't.

—CLASSIFIED AD
Weekly World News

I named all my dogs with my heart but I always named my cats for themselves.

—MURPHY KALL

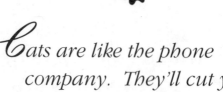

Cats are like the phone company. They'll cut you off if you won't play by their rules.

—GARRISON REED

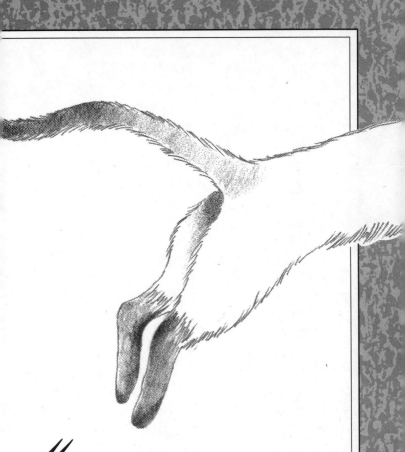

My cat is twelve inches high and as long as he wants to be.

—ROGER PRICE

*Dogs bury bones.
Cats hide thoughts.*

—IRWIN SEPTIMUS

*Cats allow us to have it
their way.*

—AUSTIN HUNTER

*Your cat is always in the last
place you think to look.*

—DAVID LEVY

Cats have nine lives, fleas have ten.

—BRIAN WALSH

Life is hard; then you nap.

—KATE LINDER
(Esther Valentine on
"The Young and the Restless")

If people slept as much as cats, instead of 9 to 5 we'd have noon to 1.

—TIFFANY ALETHEA YOUNG

Cats are capable of making order out of chaos and most certainly chaos out of order.

—LADY JANE WINTHROP

You can't take a cat for a
walk, and even if you could,
she'd ditch you.

—COLETTE GERARD

*K*ittens seem capable of
whistling.

—KIM LANKFORD

A cat can run away without ever leaving home.

—LISA MARSOLI

Cats never make the same mistake once.

—LEONARD STERN

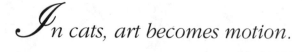

In cats, art becomes motion.

—M. MALLOY

*When the green eyes of a
cat look deep into you,
you know that whatever it
is they are saying is true.*

—LILLIAN MOORE

A cat will fetch your newspaper if there is a story in it about a mouse.

—JO MORGAN

If cats could talk, they wouldn't.

—NAN PORTER

Cats are very straightforward in the way they weasel out of responsibility.

—H. THOMAS YU

A writer without a cat risks taking himself too seriously.

—GARRISON REED

Dogs eat. Cats dine.

—ANN TAYLOR

It is comforting to have a glass of wine, a good book to read and a cat by your side...who can turn pages.

—JULIE SOMMARS

$\mathcal{Y}$ou'd sleep a lot, too, if
you had to spend nine lives
chasing mice.

—W.S.D. MILGRIM

$\mathcal{T}$here is no more luxuriant
sleep than the sleep of a cat
curled up in your lap.

—MADELYN KAMEN

Fads fade but cats are eternal.

—LYNN STACY

Cats everywhere asleep on
the shelves like motorized
bookends.

— AUDREY THOMAS

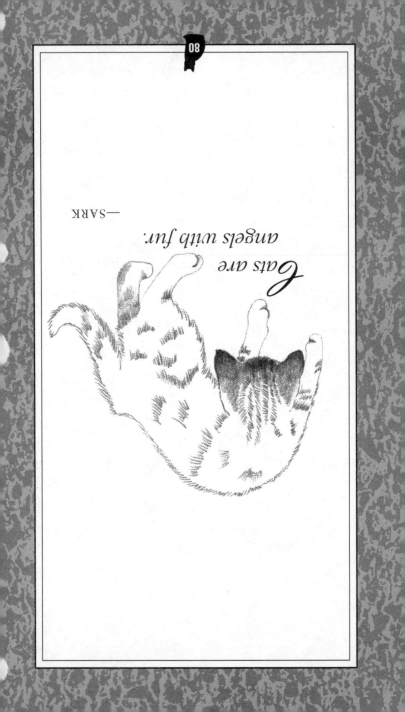

Cats are angels with fur.

—SARK